Egyptologists Guide Book For Kids

Speedy Publishing LLC
40 E. Main St. #1156
Newark, DE 19711

www.speedypublishing.com

Copyright 2014
9781635010886
First Printed October 20, 2014

 speedypublishing

Egypt Quick Facts...

Most Ancient Egyptian pyramids were built as tombs for Pharaohs and their families.

Egypt Quick Facts...

Over 130 pyramids have been discovered in Egypt. The shape of ancient Egyptian pyramids is thought to have been inspired by the spreading rays of the sun.

Egypt Quick Facts...

The first Egyptian pyramid is believed to be the Pyramid of Djoser, it was built in Saqqara around 4650 years ago (2640 BC).

Egypt Quick Facts...

The Great Pyramid of Giza is the oldest and largest of three pyramids in the Giza Necropolis.

Egypt Quick Facts...

Also known as the Pyramid of Khufu, it is the oldest of the Ancient Wonders of the World and the last one still largely intact.

Egypt Quick Facts...

Hieroglyphs were developed about 3,000 B.C. and may have started as early wall paintings. In contrast to English's 26 letters, there are more than 700 different Egyptian hieroglyphs.

Egypt Quick Facts...

The ancient Egyptians worshipped more than 1,000 different gods and goddesses. The most important god of all was Ra, the sun god.

Egypt Quick Facts...

The first pharaoh of Egypt is considered to be King Menes, who united the Upper and Lower Kingdoms in 3150 B.C. He named the capital of the united lands Memphis, which means "Balance of Two Lands." Legend says he ruled for 60 years until he was killed by a hippopotamus.

Egypt Quick Facts...

Ancient Egyptians mummified not only people but animals as well. Archeologists discovered a 15 ft. (4.5m) long mummified crocodile. The crocodile is known as the "devourer of human hearts" in the ancient Book of the Dead.

Egypt Quick Facts...

The ancient Egyptians were the first people to have a year consisting of 365 days divided into 12 months. They also invented clocks.

Egypt Quick Facts...

The ancient Egyptians believed that the god Thoth invented writing and passed its secret to humans. His symbols were a bird called an ibis and a baboon.

Egypt Quick Facts...

The giant sphinx guarding the three pyramids of Giza is thought to represent the pharaoh Khafre (Chephren), son of Khufu. Sphinxes are generally believed to have been built to guard tombs.

Egypt Quick Facts...

Ancient Egyptians believed that mummification ensured the deceased a safe passage to the afterlife. The mummification process had two stages: first the embalming of the body, then the wrapping and burial of the body. Organs were stored in canopic jars, each jar representing a god.

NO PHOTO INSIDE
THE TEMPLE

Egypt Quick Facts...

In 2011, archeologists discovered an enormous statue of the ancient Egyptian pharaoh Amenhotep III (grandfather of Tutankhamen). One of the largest statues ever found, it was actually first discovered in 1923 and then rehidden.

Egypt Quick Facts...

The word pharaoh began as a nickname for the Egyptian king. It means "great house" because everyone believed the king's human body was home to a god. The term wasn't actually used until the 20th dynasty (1185-1070 B.C.).

Egypt Quick Facts...

A priest often wore the jackal-headed mask of the god Anubis when making a body into a mummy. Ancient Egyptians associated Anubis (the god of the death) with jackals because jackals would uncover bodies from Egyptian cemeteries and eat them.

Egypt Quick Facts...

Egypt's Nile River is the world's longest, running 4,135 miles (6,670 km). Ancient Egyptians would measure the depth of the Nile using a "nilometer." The English word "Nile" is derived from the Semitic nahal, meaning "river." Ancient Egyptians called the river iteru, meaning "great river."

Egypt Quick Facts...

Ancient Egyptians believed the tears of the goddess Isis made the Nile overflow each year. They celebrated the flood with a festival called the "Night of the Tear Drop."

Printed in Great Britain
by Amazon.co.uk, Ltd.,
Marston Gate.